About Starters Facts

This colorful new range of information books encourages young readers to find out things for themselves. The text is graded into three reading levels — red, blue, and green. As well as providing a valuable source of reference, the books encourage further interest in the topic through activities and puzzles.

Accompanying each FACTS book is a STARTERS STORY, which uses the same topic as the starting point for an exciting story.

For those interested in planes, **Airport** is linked to an exciting STARTERS STORY called **Flight into Danger.**

Reading Consultants

Betty Root, Tutor-in-charge, Center for the Teaching of Reading, University of Reading.

Geoffrey Ivimey, Senior Lecturer in Child Development, University of London Institute of Education.

Airport

illustrated by
Juliet Stanwell Smith

Starters Facts • Green 1

We are going to the airport. We are going
to meet Aunt Jane and Uncle Pete. They
live abroad, and are going to stay with
us for three weeks.

2

We want to have a look around the airport. We are leaving early, so that we can see all the planes before Aunt Jane and Uncle Pete arrive.

3

This large building is the passenger
terminal. It is where people go to catch
their planes. Other people arrive here
from abroad. This is where we are going
to meet Uncle Pete and Aunt Jane.

4

The passenger terminal is very busy.
Some people are asking questions at the
information desk. Big boards show the
times of flights arriving at the airport and
those departing from it.

These departing passengers are
checking in. Their tickets are checked at
the airline desk. The man weighs their
luggage and sticks labels on it, so that it
does not get lost.

6

The luggage is taken away on a moving belt. Now it is ready to be put in the plane. The man shows the passengers which way to go.

passport
check

security
check

Passengers who are going abroad must
take their passports with them. Their
passports are checked. Security officers
search bags and pockets for guns and
bombs. This security check is to stop
hijacking.

At some airports passengers walk out
to the plane. At other airports they go in
buses. Here the passengers go to the
plane along a covered walkway called a
pier. An air hostess says hello.

runway

IBERIA

Trident

Alitalia

Boeing 727

Airbus

AIR FRANCE

10

Tristar

hangars

DC9

DC8

SWISSAIR

AIR CANADA

Concorde

British airways

air traffic
control

In the passenger terminal there is a
large window. From here you can see
the airport and the buildings. You can
see big jets on the runway. Each airline
paints its jets in different colors.

tail

food

luggage

jet
engine

fuel

This jet is getting ready to take off. Food
and drink are put on board. Passengers'
luggage is put in the hold. The hold is
also loaded up with cargo.

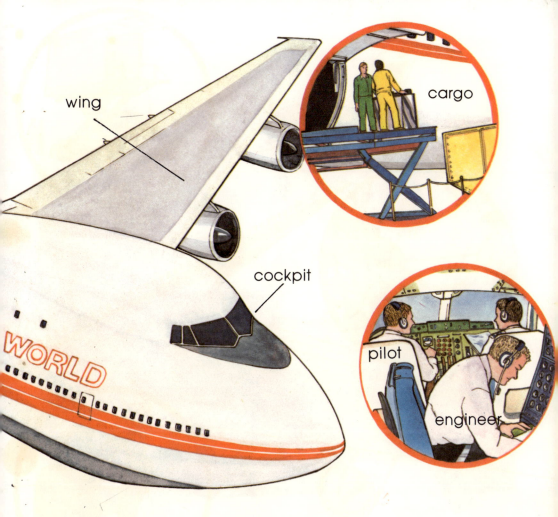

wing

cargo

cockpit

pilot

engineer

Boeing 747
Jumbo

The tanks are filled with fuel. The pilots
and the engineers check the instruments
in the cockpit. The plane is now ready
to take off.

The passengers are in their seats. The
pilot talks to air traffic control on his
radio. The controller looks at her radar
screen. She can see if it is safe and
clear for the plane to take off.

14

A tractor pushes the huge plane
forward. The plane then goes to the top
of the runway and moves away. With a
mighty roar, the plane speeds down the
runway and climbs into the air.

jet
engine

All the planes must be kept safe. Around
the airport are the hangars. This is
where the engineers check all the parts
of the planes. They mend any part that is
broken. These engineers are checking a
jet engine.

16

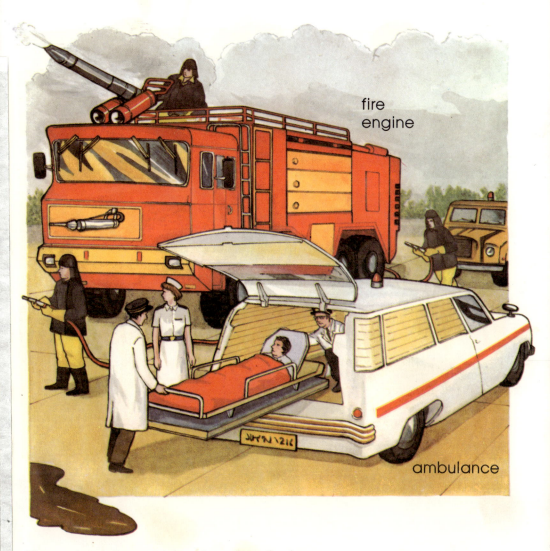

fire
engine

ambulance

The airport must be kept safe too.
Airports have special fire engines. They
can shoot foam at high speed, to put out
fires. If a plane is in danger, fire engines
and ambulances rush to the runway.

It is time for Aunt Jane and Uncle Pete's flight to arrive. Here comes their plane now. It is following the red lights on the ground. The pilot is talking to air traffic control on the radio.

Touchdown! The huge plane lands on the
runway. The jet engines go into reverse
to slow the plane down.

This is the ramp serviceman. He signals
to the pilot and shows him where to park
the jet. The jet engines are very noisy. The
ramp serviceman keeps his ears covered.

Uncle Pete and Aunt Jane leave the plane and
a bus takes them to the passenger terminal.
The man checks their passports.
Their luggage is taken off the plane
and brought to the terminal.

customs

luggage

Uncle Pete and Aunt Jane pick up their luggage. They take it through customs. The customs people check their bags.

Here they come, now! They are carrying
their luggage. Aunt Jane has a present
for us both. It is a model jet, just like the
ones we have seen.

Airport Activities

Make an airport
from paper and cardboard.
Do you have any model planes?
Keep them on the runway.

1. Take a large sheet of
newspaper. Paint on grass
and runways as shown.

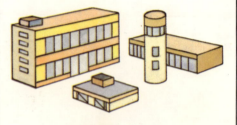

2. Cardboard boxes and
rolls can be painted to look
like airport buildings.

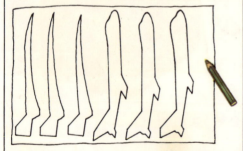

3. Trace onto cardboard six
plane shapes from page 25.

4. Cut out the plane shapes
and color in both sides.

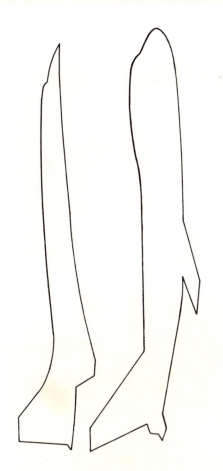

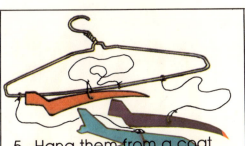

5. Hang them from a coat hanger above the runway. Use different lengths of thread.

Airport Quiz

Look at this airport.
How many hangars can you see?
How many tractors can you see?
Where is air traffic control?
How many fire engines can you see?

Airport Puzzle

The engineers want to check these planes in the hangars. Can you put each plane in the correct hangar?

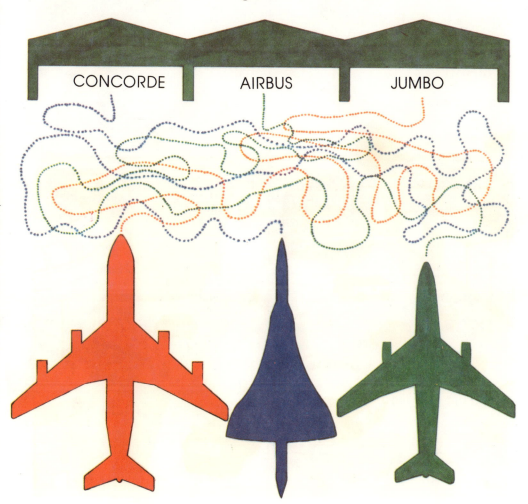

CONCORDE   AIRBUS   JUMBO

Airport Word List

passenger page 4	runway page 11
flight page 5	fuel page 12
luggage page 6	pilot page 13
passport page 8	ambulance page 17
jet page 11	ramp serviceman page 20

Each information book is linked to a story in the new **Starters** program. Both kinds of book are graded into progressive reading levels — red, blue, and green. Titles in the program include:

Starters Facts

RED 1: Going to the Zoo
RED 2: Birds
RED 3: Clowns
RED 4: Going to the Hospital
RED 5: Going to School

BLUE 1: Space Travel
BLUE 2: Cars
BLUE 3: Dinosaurs
BLUE 4: Christmas
BLUE 5: Trains

GREEN 1: Airport
GREEN 2: Moon
GREEN 3: Forts and Castles
GREEN 4: Stars
GREEN 5: Earth

Starters Stories

RED 1: Zoo for Sale
RED 2: The Birds from Africa
RED 3: Sultan's Elephants
RED 4: Rosie's Hospital Story
RED 5: Danny's Class

BLUE 1: The Space Monster
BLUE 2: The Red Racing Car
BLUE 3: The Dinosaur's Footprint
BLUE 4: Palace of Snow
BLUE 5: Mountain Express

GREEN 1: Flight into Danger
GREEN 2: Anna and the Moon Queen
GREEN 3: The Secret Castle
GREEN 4: The Lost Starship
GREEN 5: Nuka's Tale

First published 1980 by
Macdonald Educational Ltd.,
Holywell House,
Worship Street,
London EC2

© Macdonald Educational Ltd. 1980

ISBN 0-382-06488-7
Published in the United States by
Silver Burdett Company
Morristown, New Jersey
1980 Printing

Library of Congress
Catalog Card No. 80-52521

1 2 3 4 5 6 7 8 9 10—CAD—85 84 83 82 81 80

Editor: Philip Steele
Teacher Panel: Susan Alston, Susan Batten, Ann Merriman, Julia Rickell, Gwen Trier
Subject Consultant: Henry Adler
Production: Rosemary Bishop